PARENTING FROM WITHIN

The Enlightened Guide to Raising Our Children

by

K. Samsamy

ISBN: 978-0-9815109-0-3

Printed in the United States by Lightning Source

Distributed by Ingram

Cover Artwork and Design: Bahar Malek

Edited by: Janaki "Natalie" Parikh

ACKNOWLEDGEMENTS

B'ism'Allah - Invoking the name of the Creator, Most High, Most Benevolent

Truly, thanks for the type of contributions that led to the coalescence of this project cannot be given in words. The words here then, may only point towards the essence received from the individuals, for which the author is most thankful.

First and foremost to "Medium K" – not for doing, but just for being, as you are the fundamental inspiration for this text.

To all who contributed to this book, Natalie, Mike, and my lovely wife Spring – your support is the water that made this flower bloom.

And last, certainly not least, to Andreas, who was the vehicle through which this book made it to the press, and therefore the fuel that made the project go. Without you, this would never have been possible.

Table of Contents

Prologue

This book was not written by the author alone, but rather, in conjunction with the universal life force that bonds all parents throughout space and time. Indeed, the words that you will read in these pages could very well have been written by you, the parent, and as such, this book is less of a "how-to" parenting book, and more of a glimpse into that part of your eternal soul that has chosen, for this lifetime on the Earth plane, to experience the wonders and joys of parenting. Take only from this book what you feel resonates with you at the time you are reading it, for again, it is after all your words too.

...

Introduction

Parents are spiritual guides to their children.

Initially, you are either intimidated by or appreciative of the divine right that you have chosen to become a spiritual guide for your children. Regardless of which is your natural reaction, it is a strong reaction no doubt, for choosing to become a parent is one of the most fundamental human experiences that a soul can choose. And for this reason, the choice carries a huge impact, both emotionally in this lifetime, and in the karmic wavelength for your soul in the eternal universe.

This book is about redefining the very purpose of parenthood. It will delve deep into your fears, your doubts, and your disbelief. It will test your emotions, your will, and your ability to love. But then again, your child is testing you in all these aspects every day! In fact, this is why we love our children so dearly, and why the experience of being a parent is one of the most fulfilling on this Earth.

We begin with a look at the "conventional" parenting paradigm as a collection of theories and ideas; "conventional" because it may no longer serve us in this, the new age of human evolution, and indeed it hasn't truly been working for quite some time now. However, until a new paradigm surfaces that resonates more strongly than the current paradigm, there is no change. As parents, we hope to be able to find in these pages a new way, or at least some direction, that is based on love, compassion, harmony, and fearlessness. By utilizing such a love-based system, we as parents can never fail our children.

Part I

Parents as Disciplinarians

Chapter 1

Conventional Approaches

The conventional view on parenting considers the parent's primary role as that of a disciplinarian. This disciplinarian role includes the sum total of actions that involve talking to your children in a manner that can best be described as the "do this/ don't do that" consciousness.

Indeed, most parents believe that this is the essence of parenting – that their role is, essentially, to constructively guide and regulate their children's behavior, to watch over them, make sure they are OK, and, in this way, express their love for their child. The very foundation of conventional parenting, indeed, is that the better parent you are, and the more love you want to show your child, then the more involved in their lives you should be. This means that you should shower them with attention and care, discipline them "when they need it", and guide them at critical junctures in their lives. The stereotype of the uncaring, uninvolved parent is so pervasive in our collective parenting consciousness that the very definition of parental love, or the love that we give our children, has been based on this stereotype's dual opposite.

Many societies have even set up institutions to mirror this authoritarian dynamic and reinforce the parents' role as disciplinarians. The school system, where children spend large quantities of time, is a prime example. The school, where parents drop off their children every day, is sometimes even seen as an extended parenting institution, which is why parents are so concerned about choosing schools for their children.

In the end, therefore, it is out of love that parents become disciplinarians and, while the intention is well based, the attention is not necessarily so. To find out why, let's examine the intricacies of the "parents as disciplinarians" paradigm more closely. By the way, "he" and "she" will be used alternately throughout the text but it is always assumed that children of both genders are included.

The role of a parent in this mindset is primarily to:

- Discipline the child in order to protect him.

Typically, this means protecting the child by watching out for him and intervening when the child is putting himself in danger.

- Discipline the child to teach her "right and wrong."

Definitions of right and wrong will vary among individuals and families but, in general, this approach tends to foster discipline as a means to teach the child a moral code, so that the child does not later in life do something "wrong" or "bad" and thus bring harm to herself.

- Discipline the child in order to teach the child about life.

Usually this involves helping to integrate the child into society by making sure they learn the basics and attain a level of conformity essential for their future success.

- Manage the child's life by directing activities, friends, ideas in a "positive direction."

But in fact, the disciplinarian mindset is in actuality caused by the *parent's fear and future projected guilt.* In reality, discipline breeds dependency and discourages self-regulation. Considering that self-regulation is the first step towards self-evolution, the disciplinarian paradigm actually limits our children's spiritual growth and human development. Let's examine how this works.

Chapter 2

Parental Fear

It is the parents' job to protect their child.

This has become such a common parenting thought pattern that it could be the essence of a "parenting 101" class, if one were to exist. From the very moment a man and woman discover that they will become parents, society, doctors, etc. are all conveying the message that one of our most basic jobs as parents is to "protect" this new being from the big, bad world at large and, indeed, suggesting that this is our most primary role as parents. This mindset has been so effectively ingrained into humanity that many parents feel a "natural instinct", a protective streak towards their children that is deep-rooted in their emotional consciousness.

But in deeper reality, this mindset is *actually rooted in fear-based thinking* and any "natural instincts" as such are leftovers from our evolutionary history as animals in the predator-filled wild. So let's start from the very foundation of this belief system. If the parent's job is to protect the child, and the method used is discipline, then what exactly is the parent protecting the child from? This assumes that there are no more lions, tigers and bears out there, at least not where most of us live!

The typical answer is to protect the child from "outside influences", or "things outside my child's control." This may be true in terms of a material perception of our world but, in deeper reality, it goes against the most basic fabric of our universe and its laws.

Your child's soul is attracting everything into his own life, as indeed all of us are. Therefore nothing actually "happens" to your child; rather, your child makes everything "happen" to himself. For our souls are created of the same cosmic matter as the Higher Power, the One that creates all that is. Therefore, on the micro-level of our own lives, *we* act as the ultimate maestro, for we are created of the Master's very essence. Indeed, it has now been scientifically established through the study of quantum physics that we live, essentially, in a thought-based universe and that the nature of those thoughts control our experience of reality.

So then, let's get back to the discipline part. If your child is the maestro of her own life, then by disciplining your child in order to protect her, what are you, in deeper reality, protecting her from? Herself. And then by attempting to protect your child from himself, the disciplinarian paradigm is actually *breaking the connection between the child's conscious mind and his higher self.* By interfering in this most basic communication, the child is missing out on some of the most crucial pathways and neural connections that her brain will make in her lifetime.

Let's use a simple example. Say that a young child is fascinated with the stove. He is always around the stove when his parents are cooking, and constantly wants to be involved. The parents, however, realizing that the child may burn his hand, constantly discipline the child, saying, "No, you shouldn't touch the stove", or "Stay away from that." The principle of "disciplining the child in order to protect the child" is very clearly at work here. Furthermore, this seems like sound, obvious, basic parenting. But, on a deeper level, realizing the likely root cause of this parenting behavior, we may arrive at a different conclusion.

Is the motivating factor behind the parent's action truly concern for the child's wellbeing? It would seem so, but in fact this is not the case. For the child, remember, is coming from a source of infinite wisdom. In addition, the child's soul attracts everything that the child needs into her life in order to grow and develop into an adult capable of fulfilling that soul's particular higher purpose. So, if the only way that soul can learn a particular lesson is to get 3rd degree burns on her body and be taken to the hospital, that soul will find a way to create that reality eventually, whether the parents discipline the child or not. Perhaps later, as an adult, she will get into a car accident at a time when her body is less able to heal itself and so the lesson must be learned harder. Or later the individual may become deformed or otherwise have massive physical difficulties from learning that same lesson that, as a child, would have been much easier to learn.

In addition, disciplining the child in order to protect the child from his own self presupposes that your child does not inherently know how to protect himself already! Being that all humans are imbued with infinite consciousness, like all things in the universe, it is actually *impossible* for your child to "not know" something. The only issue is

9

how well your child can *connect* to that part of his being that *is* the infinite source of knowledge, so that the knowledge can be brought into the conscious mind and used in everyday life.

In addition, a child is less removed from universal consciousness because she has spent less time on the Earth plane and away from infinity. If anything, children are wiser than adults just by virtue of the fact that they are naturally less disconnected from their higher selves, for they have spent fewer years on this Earth plane as incarnated beings focusing on mundane, material form issues. (Or, in human terms, they are younger.)

However, looking at it from the perspective of the parent's fear, it is easy to see why disciplining the child for the child's protection has become a bastion of common parenting techniques. For if the parents, on a deeper level, know that the child is safe to begin with, and by the very nature of that child's infinite consciousness can protect himself, then what is the actual root cause of the parent's disciplinary action?

It is the parents' fear of the child coming to harm, and the associated future guilt that would be felt with that outcome. Said simply, it is the parent's selfishness that is the true motivation. If the child comes to harm, the natural emotional reaction of the parent will be concern, despair, and later, guilt. Guilt that they "allowed" their child to come to harm and that they somehow should have done better. Fear of feeling these negative feelings motivates the parents to discipline the child in the manner described in the "hand and hot stove" example.

In fact, if the parent does have a lot of fear, the child's soul may *purposely injure itself* simply to *teach the parent to deal with and resolve that fear.* This is because the child loves the parent, and the child's higher self realizes that the parent needs assistance in dealing with this fear. So, out of love, the child's soul obliges in a manner of self-sacrifice that is typical of the compassion of infinite consciousness, or God, where the child just came from.

Therefore, from a spiritual perspective, *fear of your children harming themselves by touching the stove,* along with a constant focus on this matter, *may actually cause your children to become seriously injured by touching the stove!* Such is the deeper reality of living in a thought-based universe.

Because in deeper reality, by removing the fear from the equation, it is a less than one-in-a-million chance that massive harm will come to the child by touching the stove. In the worst case, the child will quickly pull her hand away, cry for some short amount of time, and have a slight burn on the hand that will likely heal completely within days or weeks. But what a valuable lesson they will have learned, on their own, to help their soul and human spirit grow!

More than that, given children's erratic behavior, sudden movements, and the inability of a parent to stay focused on the child 100% percent of the time, is it truly possible (other than by removing the stove from your house) to entirely limit the child's ability to get near enough to the stove to reach out and, possibly, burn their hand? It is not possible, neither physically nor metaphysically.

Truly, all that is required is for the parent to turn his or her head, and the child may touch the stove. Or, for the parent to lose focus for even one second, which is only human, and there goes your child's hand towards the stove. It is an *illusion* and a game we play with ourselves as parents to think that we can somehow control our child's actions and influence them through power or force, even actions that we feel will bring massive harm to our child.

So what can we do as parents instead? Remember, we live in a thought-based universe, composed of essence and spirit, with the material world being only the manifestation of our inner feelings. Therefore, by removing from your parenting reality the fear of your child coming to harm, you are at least not creating the very circumstance you fear. Thus, the child will likely not ever burn his hand on the stove. And if the child does, it is because she chose to – and your job as a parent is simply to help them understand why they chose to, and give them your love in every step of their own personal learning process.

This simple example of the hand and the hot stove may seem silly and, of course, the intent here is NOT to advise parents to let their children run loose in the streets in front of moving cars, or simply ignore all harm and danger that comes the child's way.

The purpose here is to understand, accept, honor, and *let go of the fear in your heart as a parent.* By doing so, you liberate yourself and your child. Then, *without fear,* your role in protecting your child will become that of a guide, not a disciplinarian. In this way, you will allow your wisdom and intuition to take over and properly guide your child for whatever unique situations your child's soul has chosen to experience in this lifetime.

Most importantly, expand this example to include other actions in your parenting life. Consider what other less life-threatening situations exist with your child for which your primary motivation for disciplining your child has been a desire to protect him or her from something?

Make a list, right now – take out a pen and paper and do it.

Finished?

Well congratulations, you are now staring at all the fears to erase in your parenting heart in order to become a better parent!

Making such a list is the first step in dealing with these fears. And, dealing with these fears will be the single greatest gift you can give your child.

Therefore, looking at the situation on a deeper level, one begins to see that the sum effect of this notion of discipline as a form of protecting the child actually has the converse effect in the long run. More importantly, there are other, more enlightened ways of parenting that we will explore.

Chapter 3

Right-and-Wrong Constructs

Before exploring the specific effects of a "right versus wrong" system on discipline and parenting, let's first examine briefly the effects of a right-versus-wrong system on human society in general. While this may easily form the topic of an entire book, I will provide a short summary below.

More than discipline, the fundamental issue here is our very conception of right and wrong. Indeed, let's stop and ask for a moment, where does the notion of right and wrong come from? Is it inherent in our nature? Is it embedded in our most spiritual text? In fact, neither of these is true. The notion of right and wrong, in fact, is a learned behavior and a societal construct.

Do you doubt this statement? That's natural. The notion of right and wrong has been the foundational principle upon which the majority of human civilizations have been built (at least in the modern era). It has served its purpose, but it is a less evolved concept than other forms by which we may guide human behavior, and the behavior of our children.

The conceptualization of right and wrong rests, at its root, on one primary fallacy – that the self is not 100% responsible for everything that the self experiences. Or, said in another way, that you are not 100% responsible for everything in your life.

In all systems of right and wrong, there is a set of principles not created by the self, that the self must adhere to nonetheless. Whether this system is created in the name of religion or morals, the foundational principle is that there is a set of rules, classifying all human behavior into either "right" or "wrong" categories. In addition, these rules are taken as immutable authorities or, if they do change, they must be changed by whoever created them (the church, e.g.). At its core, then, this form of belief puts the responsibility for the individual's actions, at least partially, in another's control.

The right-and-wrong construct is seemingly such a basic fundamental for so many people that it is difficult to perceive any other system through which humans can live their lives. In fact, not only is there a better system, but the system of right and wrong is actually in conflict with the most basic construct of the universe! This is because the universe itself (the stars, planets, sun, Earth, your shoes, and your children) has been and is being created by us, every minute of every day.

We live in a thought-based universe, and we are the co-creators of our world. By understanding and accepting that you create your reality and, through your individual contribution, you play a constant, active role in creating the entire universe, it means you are taking 100% responsibility for everything that you create – not just what you do, *but what happens to you as well!* Furthermore, you would naturally come to the conclusion that, if you create everything that you do and everything that happens to you, then in fact you are in 100% complete control of your own life – everything, all of it.

This is, of course, an extremely scary scenario for many. Why?

Because if you knew for a fact that you created everything in your life, it would mean you would have to take 100% responsibility for all the things in your life. This would include the things you perceive as "bad" or "wrong" in your life, including the actions of others towards you, the state of the world (war, poverty, and hunger, if that is part of your reality), the culture you live in, the money you make, the people who are your birth-family, and so on. Everything, your whole world, your whole experience, all of it.

So then, what does this say about you? If you created all these "bad" things," are you a "bad person"? If you are 100% completely responsible for the traffic accident last month, the fight with your mother yesterday, your bad hair days, your drug addictions, your depression, your anxiety, your stress, your financial situation... Magnify this line of thinking to every single thing you think is wrong or bad with your life and the universe, and it is easy to see how many of us would be filled with a sense of utmost depression and hopelessness with this worldview, which is why the system of right and wrong was created.

It was created because the "right versus wrong" system teaches us that many of these things are *outside of our control.* Our job on this Earth is simply to adhere to the rules, be a good person, and some other force in the universe (usually God) will take care of the rest. This is much easier than a world where we are 100% responsible for everything in our reality!

Thus the system of right and wrong, in fact, *protects us from ourselves.* It "protects" us by forming a veil between our selves and our true responsibilities, watering down that responsibility to a simple equation of conformance to a set of pre-determined rules whose origin sits outside of our selves, whether religious or not.

However, in doing so, this worldview also *disconnects us from our higher selves* and thus it hinders our evolution and blocks us from achieving higher levels of consciousness.

Now that we understand the basic problems with the overall system of right and wrong, let's apply this understanding to our focus on parenting.

What are we, as parents, doing by disciplining our children based on a system of right and wrong? We are simply *reinforcing this outdated belief system in our children, and helping to disconnect them from their higher selves.* It doesn't matter what you specifically say is right and wrong, or whether you are using a religious perspective or a secular one. The entire discipline system based on the right-and-wrong worldview sees the parent's job as teaching the child about this system using the method of discipline. When the child does something "right", we reward him; when the child does something "wrong", she is punished. This becomes true regardless of exactly *how* the parent defines right and wrong.

If we say it is wrong to watch too much TV, when our child does so, he is disciplined. And it's right to get straight A's, so our child gets a special party when she does this. It's wrong to be selfish and not share with your sibling, it's wrong to act up in class, it's wrong to disrespect your parents, it's wrong to stay out late, it's wrong to do drugs, it's wrong to have sex at a young age... and the list goes on.

For each wrong, there is a form of discipline such as grounding, taking away something from the child, etc. For each right, there is a reward, even if it's just an affirmative "good job" from the parent or, in deeper reality, the giving of more love.

So, what is the more evolved view? Well, if as an adult, your child is 100% responsible for their entire reality, it's best to teach them that from a very young age! Indeed, they are responsible for their entire realities as a child anyway.

How can this be taught? Well, the foundational principle is this: if we are not to guide human actions by a system of right and wrong, what is, then, the guide for human behavior? It is the under-standing that as 100% responsible creators of our own lives, we must deal with every element of that reality personally. Therefore, if I perform actions that will negatively affect my reality, it is I and no one else that will have to live in that negative real-ity that I created and reap the negative conse-quences. So then, the motivation is very clear why I should avoid "negative" or unenlightened behav-ior as much as possible, and not because of fear of punishment or conformance with a moral or reli-gious code so that some Almighty force may judge me more kindly at the close of my life. Rather, it is because *my behavior will create an unenlightened real-ity that I myself will then experience.* This is true of all actions, even those that I perform against others.

Ancient sages referred to this as karma. Isaac Newton discovered it millennia later as the 3rd of the Laws of Motion: *for every action, there is an equal and opposite reaction.* Or, in the modern era, we say, "What goes around comes around", which is of course a re-tread of the time-honored "You reap what you sow". The ancients' wisdom has not been implemented properly because, when per-ceived through the lens of a system based on right and wrong, the truth in the wisdom becomes dis-torted. When perceived through a worldview that says I am 100% responsible for my actions, the wisdom rings true.

So then, perceived this way, the goal of parenting is not to discipline and instill in your child the rudimentary understanding of a right-and-wrong system. Rather, it should be to assist your child in understanding the 100% responsibility reality that is, in fact, the building block of the universe. This conceptualization moves parenting from a science of parental control to the guided art of child self-control. The single most valuable lesson you can teach your child is that *they are teaching themselves their own lessons*, now and in the future, every minute of every day.

And this, indeed, involves the *withholding of traditional discipline* in order that the children come to realize that it is not mommy's or daddy's punishment that they should be concerned with, but the negative impacts in their own lives that they will experience as repercussions of their negative actions. Similarly, there is no reason to apply the dual opposite of punishment, which is reward; the universe is rewarding your child every day as a result of your child's positive actions. Your child will realize that, by focusing on her positive attributes, she will, indeed, have the power to create more of the happiness that is already being given to her. As a result of her perfect creation, this child will quickly evolve into higher and higher states of consciousness and gain the power to create anything she wants.

Rather, if they are always waiting for mommy's or daddy's reward, they will no longer have faith in themselves and their own ability to manifest reward for right action. By not seeing that they are creating their own wonderful reality through their positive attributes, they fail to focus on those positive attributes unless the parent rewards them. This instills in the child a sense that the parent, later the teacher, then the boss, the priest, the President, etc., is the source of that child's happiness because this *outside authority figure* is the source of their positive feedback for their positive actions.

Not only is this an un-evolved perspective, it is also a dangerous one. Do we now see how historical figures such as Hitler and Stalin were able to marshal enormous amounts of manpower to use to their own ends, seemingly blinding millions to their negative energies? It is because all of these people grew up with the belief system that right-and-wrong is defined by someone *outside their own selves,* that life's expectation is to follow this system to the best of your ability, and that reward and punishment comes from an *extended parent authority figure.* And the basis of this was their upbringing as children, when the parent disciplined them based on a system of right and wrong, a system rooted in the belief that control resides outside of the self.

The example is a bit harsh, but it serves to illustrate the point. Your single greatest gift to your children is assisting them in connecting with their higher selves. Discipline based on a system of right and wrong accomplishes the exact opposite – it creates a fundamental, major blockage between your children and their higher selves.

Instead, as parents we can nourish our children's relationship with their higher selves by shifting our own perceptions, ceasing to act out a system of punishment and reward, and assisting children to recognizing their own divinity.

RIGHT-AND-WRONG
PARENT CHECKLIST

Learning this can be hard at first. Until your own perceptions as a human being are shifted, it will be difficult to implement a non-disciplinarian system with your children. This checklist may help.

When your child does something "wrong":

1. Affirm to yourself, out loud if you have to, "there is no right and wrong, there is only intention and karmic consequence/action and reaction". Do this several times.

2. Check to see where your child's actions fit within your own "moral code" of right and wrong, and look for its root source. Is it something your parents taught you when you were a child? A religious belief? A societal norm? Identify the root cause of your personal coloration of your child's actions as "wrong", and make a note of it.

3. Resist the urge to judge and punish. Instead, wait for an opportune time (without anger) to talk to you child and gently guide them, by dropping hints or pointing them in the direction of

what potential karmic consequence may occur as a result of their action. Each parent does this differently.

4. Try to avoid using the word "wrong", thinking the word "wrong", or in any way acting differently around your child because of the action they performed. Instead, look at it as "action and feedback" coming from the Universe, and simply reaffirm to yourself that the Universe and your child's higher self will provide your child with the necessary feedback to grow and learn.

When your child does something "right":

1. Affirm to yourself, out loud if you have to, "there is no right and wrong, there is only intention and karmic consequence/action and reaction". Do it several times.

2. Resist the immediate temptation to reward your child. Remember, we live in a thought-based universe, so even thinking or telepathically sending "extra" love to your child begins to formulate a system of external joy in your child instead of self-reliance. Instead, look at the "right" action as simply an opportunity to re-affirm the love you already have for your child, and the reflection of divinity that you see in their action. Later, if you feel a true heart-felt conviction to provide your child

with a reward, do so, but only if it aligns with the highest purpose of your child's actions.

3. Say something to your child, in your own mind, to the order of, "This particular beautiful action that you have done is simply an outward manifestation of the inner beauty that is eternally present within you, that you control, and that nobody can take away from you". Express it out loud as well by finding a way to say this in a manner that your child can understand.

4. Make a mental note of what your child has done. When the positive karmic consequences of your child's actions show up in the material world (which it must do by karmic and universal law), mention it to yourself, and even gently to your child, especially if they do not notice it themselves.

5. Most importantly, show gratitude. Thank the Universe and your child, out loud if you can, for sharing this act of beauty with you.

Chapter 4

Success and Your Perfect Child

In the conventional parenting paradigm, we are taught that the child comes to us in raw form to be sculpted and molded, by parents, into a final form, capable of integrating into society. Indeed, one of the greatest joys of parenting is to see your child grow up and go on to accomplish great things in the world. Therefore, we want to give our kids the best chance to succeed, which includes providing them with material, emotional, and physical support in order to "make it". This thought pattern may either come from a place of fear that the child will fail and that the parents will bear that responsibility, or from a place of genuine love for the child. For the present discussion, the actual source of the thought process is irrelevant.

Because, again, the very foundational principle must be called into question – that the child comes to us in raw form, somehow imperfect, and only achieves perfection through our influence as parents. Furthermore, the conventional belief tells us that, in this raw form, the child is incapable of integrating successfully into society, and hence must be taught how to do so, whether this comes from the school system or the parents. The understanding, in sum, is that the child's future success is in large part due to her "upbringing", which is in large part due to the actions of the child's parents. That's a lot of pressure on us parents - to be responsible, at least partially, for another entity's future success? As we have now seen from previous chapters, this line of thinking is inherently flawed, for no one is responsible for another's health, wealth and happiness.

Let's deal with the first issue: does your child come to you in raw form, with the need to be sculpted and molded in order to achieve finished form? This is not possible, for everything in the universe is, at all times, created perfectly by the one Higher Power. It may not be beautiful from our current perception, but it is perfect, for it has all come from the Higher Source. If God is truly omnipresent and omnipotent, how can there be anything but perfection in the world that emanates from this universal source?

The only logical conclusion is that it is our *perception* that makes the world imperfect to us. Put another way, our thoughts and energies are what block our own reality from merging with the infinite source, and thus, becoming living perfection. In the same way, it is our perception of our children that creates their imperfections, for your children in actuality are perfect as created. Yes, even when they are crying, yelling, screaming, or throwing a tantrum, they are perfect in the eyes of the Universe and require none of your discipline. Indeed, your child was given *everything* that he needs to accomplish his higher purpose when born. There is nothing missing, nothing extra, and nothing wrong. Therefore, there is no reason to discipline your child in order to mold her or guide him to a more perfected way of being.

However - since, as parents, we were taught that we must mold and sculpt the child, our brains will affirm this belief. Since we live in a thought-based universe where action follows thought, and form follows essence, we end up unconsciously looking for things that are "wrong" in our children so that we can "fix" them. In the process, we feel useful as parents because we are "doing our job well." We actually create imperfections out of thin air by interpreting things about our child as imperfect when, in deeper reality, these are just individual aspects of our children. Oftentimes, the brain uses old experiences to craft these imaginary imperfections and the most common source for us to draw upon is our own childhood experiences.

In this way, at a completely unconscious level, we *actually create imperfections in our children* when none exist in reality. Through our perception and subsequent action towards our children, we are encouraging them to believe in this perceived imperfection themselves. Once the child *believes* that they possess this imperfection, it is manifested in their reality through their thoughts and, in this way, the *imperfection actually comes into being in the universe*. And so, ironically, through this system of trying to help our children become more perfect, we are *in actuality helping them to create their imperfections!*

How can we step out of this cycle and create a positive approach? The first step is simple – tell your child that they are perfect as created, and believe it in your own heart. Think about it – did anyone ever tell you, when you were growing up, that you were perfect as created because you were created from the universal higher source? Not likely. How would this affirmation have affected you? Go back to your own childhood memories and think of an aspect of yourself that you were told was imperfect. How would it have made you feel if your parents, instead, had reinforced your complete perfection? Has that childhood issue turned into a major issue in your adult life? Has the issue caused you pain and trauma in your adult relationships?

What greater unbounded possibilities could you have accomplished in your life to date if you had received this affirmation every day? What if, daily, someone you love had told you, without any ego or conceit but from a place of true understanding and love, that you were created perfectly. What if they said that you possessed as your *birthright* all you would ever need to accomplish your dreams, that you only needed to have faith and trust in yourself to accomplish whatever your heart desired.

Indeed one of the greatest gifts you can give your children is to acknowledge their perfection. This is like giving your children a key to an infinite source of self-power and self-realization. The root of all human problems is the disconnection between our conscious mind and our higher self, or the link between "man and God." Just planting the idea in your children's minds that they may be perfect as created will immediately call their higher selves into their conscious mind, and work wonders in your children's lives.

In communicating this reality with your child, first let go of fear and of ego. This is not a call to turn your child into some earthly Princess/Prince where you constantly shower your child's ego with gifts and lavish treatment because they are "perfect." Rather, we are speaking here of connecting with your child on a deeper plane and speaking of a universal perfection that is not bound to the ebb and flow of life events, like ego is. You do not need to give your child anything, like extra attention or material possessions, in order to prove his perfection. In fact, doing so only fosters dependency in your child on a gift-giver outside of his self. Instead, the thought and energy you convey, without any "additives or preservatives", will help awaken your child's higher self. That is the difference – the way of eternal, unconditional perfection.

Now let's deal with the second and related point, that without strict parental guidance, we believe the child is incapable on their own of integrating into society or, said another way, of becoming successful. As parents, we are so afraid of our children not becoming successful, primarily because we feel we are mostly responsible for that success.

Out of our misguided love and desire for our children to succeed, we feel that we must help them establish a minimum level of conformity within our society. Otherwise, how will they be successful? So, we discipline our child when she doesn't conform to the expectations, when he doesn't excel in school, when they act in a manner different from established societal norms, etc.

Indeed, so many common-view parenting guides, reinforced by modern psychology, state that the early years of a child's life and the way the parents raise the child seriously affect the child's ability to function and succeed in society as an adult.

While this may or may not be true, what's missing here is the understanding that all of this is your child's responsibility. Your child's soul is attracting all of these elements into his life, even from before birth. Your child's soul chose to come to you with *complete knowledge* of your situation – the financial, family, material, physical, emotional, and spiritual aspects of you and your family. Your child chose to be born in a family with exactly your circumstances, because those circumstances are exactly what your child's soul needs in order to transcend into higher states of consciousness.

Therefore, your responsibility in this aspect is far more limited than conventional parenting portrays. Instead of the worry of not providing your child "enough" or the fear that your child will grow up and not be "successful", try to start with reinforcing, everyday, what you know you have and what you know you can give your child. More than likely, that is exactly what your child needs and indeed the reason they chose you as their parents! Lose the fear of not "giving enough" to your child, for operating on that fear may drive you to hold back even what you originally have.

Bear in mind that, even if your child perceives what you can give at that time as negative, if it comes from a place of true, deep understanding of your own higher purpose as a parent, then rest assured, it is exactly the gift your child needs to receive at that moment in their personal development. They will realize it themselves in due time.

Within this perspective, bombarding your child with material and emotional attention, especially if this is outside of your means to provide, becomes pointless. There is truly no need to put your child into advanced tutoring and millions of sports classes for fear that, if you don't do these things, your child won't be successful in the future.

After all, you have no idea what your child's soul regards as successful, or what lessons they need to learn. So the entire concept of helping your child to "succeed" by showering them with what *you believe* is necessary for their success is working from a misplaced understanding.

Accept that your child is now perfect, and realize that they will be in the future. Your job as a parent is primarily to work on *seeing that perfection, not on creating it*! For there is nothing to create to achieve perfection and whatever further perfection does need to be created, your child will do on her own.

At the minimum, let the child ask before you give, and then give only what is within your higher purpose. Even not giving the child what he wants, because you don't have it, may be the lesson he needs to learn in order to be motivated to seek his desires through another medium. I am not suggesting that you withhold things from your children – far from it – because, indeed, this can be borne of the same misunderstanding. Many parents withhold money from their children in the belief that it will make them stronger, as the children must learn to make money independently. This is misguided and wrought in fear-based thinking.

Why would you need to make your child stronger, when your child is already as strong as she needs to be? From what future mistakes are you trying to rescue your child, when your child can never make a mistake, if aligned with his higher purpose?

What I am suggesting is to first let your child define their own terms of success, and then you as the parent accept it fully, without your own ideas or prejudices coloring this perception. And then, wait until your child asks for your assistance in achieving his own definition of success before you decide that, as the child's parent, you are meant to assist him in achieving that success. Consider this: you may constantly want to give your child a good schooling, and yet, perhaps she was meant to drop out of school or college, only to start a computer company that would one day invent a new communication system that would revolutionize the entire human race. And so, at age 16, your child comes and asks you for $5,000 to start a computer business. Do you color this request with your own perceptions of success? Or do you trust that you have raised your child in a way that has allowed him to connect to his higher purpose and, indeed, this is just the next step in his personal evolution towards fulfilling this destiny?

Most importantly, at all times, perceive your children as perfect just the way they are. That energy will allow your children to do the same, creating a confidence and sense of purpose that will allow them to create their own success in whatever higher purpose they pursue in their lives.

So you see, helping your child to accept and understand her own perfection will indeed give her a direct connection to the higher source. With this power, your child can manifest any success he wishes, anything. In this way, you are, in actuality helping your child to achieve success, but through a more enlightened perspective.

SUCCESS SHEET

Here is a good 3-step mantra that can be chanted or prayed, to help parents deal with the issue of their child's future success:

1 - "Whatever my child's purpose and success in life, my job is only to accept it. In this way, my child shall learn self-trust, and I shall learn the acceptance of others, which shall lead to self-acceptance."

2 – "My child is already successful, s/he just needs to find it. In helping my child to do so, I will learn to see the success I already have within myself."

3 – "My child's idea of success is so powerful it will create his/her own world to perfectly house that success. By witnessing this, I can learn to reformulate my own world to fit my inherent success, instead of the other way around."

Chapter 5

Parents as CEOs

As parents, we sometimes feel like managers or even CEOs, organizing our children's lives, managing the influences with which they come into contact, and being the gatekeeper to all that they experience. A common parental perception is that we are our child's life manager more than our child's caretaker. Conventional parenting teaches parents to monitor our children's lives, to guide and direct our children's lives at a young age when the children are supposedly incapable of making important decisions, and serving as a "filter" between the child and the outside world. We are to keep out what is "bad" and let in only what is "good" and, of course, the method to achieve this is discipline.

This monitoring and managing behavior includes monitoring friends, influence from the mass media, the child's activities, etc. This becomes even more relevant and more intensive as the child gets older, reaches the pre-teen and then teenage years, usually some of the most rocky experiences between a parent and child.

By taking a step back, we can examine where the notion of parents as children's life-managers even originated.

1.   First and foremost, there is the idea that the parents, due to their life experiences, know more than their children, or at least they have been through it before. So why not let the more experienced person take the helm and direct the ship?

2.   There is, furthermore, the belief that children are gullible, easily manipulated, easy to coerce, innocent, and vulnerable. Perceived this way, the parent as life manager is really a protector.

3.   And last, there is the idea that it is the parent's inherent responsibility to be the child's life manager. Indeed, we often hear of "bad parents" who let their children do whatever they want. Especially in environments where there are younger children, parents are expected to control their kids, as if they were dogs being walked in the park (perhaps leading to the "child leash" phenomenon). Very often, parents with unruly children are looked down upon by other parents and society at large.

However, at second glance, we see that these foundational principles that led to the idea of the parent as the child's life manager can be seen in a different light. Once the foundational principles are defused, the need for child-life management largely slips away.

The first point that parents, through having more life experience, know more than their kids, is not a false premise. It's just that the perspective on this statement has been lost. Parents, through spending a greater number of years physically present on the Earth plane incarnated in this lifetime (we are "older" than our children), have greater knowledge of just that – physical presence on the Earth plane in this lifetime. Important, to be sure, but the sum total of this knowledge, while it looks grand, is probably less than 10% of the total important knowledge that your child possesses or needs to learn. The other 90%, composed of emotional, spiritual, mental and metaphysical knowledge, is not dependent on time spent on the physical Earth plane but rather on the individual soul's sum total of spiritual progress.

Therefore, the parent has no authority to speak on just any subject, simply by virtue of the fact that the parent has spent greater physical time on the

Earth plane in this lifetime. Your children do not need to be constantly bombarded with what limited knowledge your extra time on this Earth plane can give them. In fact, by making this type of knowledge more important than it really is, you are disconnecting your child's link with the *other forms of knowledge* that your child may naturally possess at a higher level than even you do. Some children seem to have gifts or intuitive understandings (dare I say psychic ability?) that naturally come to them and oftentimes the parents don't understand these things at all. But by making this type of knowledge *at least equal* with mundane material Earth plane knowledge, you are encouraging your child to grow and understand their intuitive gifts and alternative forms of knowledge.

Accept this, and respect this. There is no spiritual hierarchy, and nobody is ahead of or behind anyone else. There are just different levels and everyone is exactly where they need to be at that time. So then, do you have something to teach your child about physical life on this Earth plane? Of course. Does this knowledge alone entitle you, the parent, to become the child's life manager as a result of this extra knowledge? Not so. At best, you should make decisions jointly with your child.

We move on to the second idea – that children, especially young children, are gullible, vulnerable, and easily manipulated. We established in the previous section that the child's soul is perfect as created and attracts everything into his/her life, whether it is perceived by us, the parent, as good or bad. This also means your child is infinitely strong, coming from the infinite higher source. Is not God infinitely strong? Was not your child, as were you, I, this book, and everything else, created from this higher source? All are infinitely strong.

So then, why are children believed to be vulnerable and easily manipulated? Because when a parent believes this, even during pregnancy, s/he is sending the child the energy that "you are vulnerable and I must take care of you." Indeed, the parents' very *perception of the child's supposed weakness is what creates that weakness in the child*. Because remember, once the child believes that s/he is vulnerable, gullible, and easily manipulated, this will become that child's reality, as action follows thought and belief. Whether directly or indirectly, the parents will give the child this message if they believe it in their hearts, for in that case it is the parent's reality.

Only by truly accepting your child's perfection and the way this perfection gives your child ultimate power can you break the cycle that has plagued humanity for thousands of years. It has come to a point that the word "child" even evokes feelings of innocence, weakness, and the need for protection. We use this language daily – "well he's just a child." We even have special rights and privileges for children. These are not necessarily bad things, but think about it from the child's perspective. Since they were old enough to move, they have been treated like vulnerable objects by society and their parents. No wonder most children end up believing this!

The only aspect in which the child is vulnerable is in certain aspects of the physical Earth plane. If you wish to or need to provide management and protection for your child, it is in this aspect only and, presumably, for a limited amount of time. But to make this singular issue the be-all and end-all of the perceptions surrounding your child's relationship with the outside world not only limits your child's development but also disconnects her from her higher self. If left to their own devices, children will find ways to access the other planes and dimensions of existence in order to make their way in the physical universe. Indeed, it is very possible that through manipulation of the ethereal spiritual and metaphysical energies, young children can learn to manifest their own protection in the physical Earth plane even from a very early age.

This is, again, not to say that parents have zero responsibility towards their children's lives or that there is no management to be done. The point here is that the pendulum has swung so far in the other direction that a focus on reducing parents' management of their children's lives can only help.

The final section in the chapter has to do with the parent's monitoring of the child's relationship to outside influences and the world at large. This is most fundamentally evident when the child reaches the pre-teen and teenage years, but is equally important for the child's younger years. It has become such a lightning rod for the parent-child relationship in the modern world that a little extra time will be spent on it.

First and foremost, parents must cleanse themselves of their fears and future-projected guilt in dealing with this subject. One of the major motivational factors for managing your child's life is the fear, as a parent, that your child will come to harm, whether it is emotional, physical, or mental harm. Fear of your child doing drugs or getting involved in criminal activity leads to monitoring your child's friends, social circles, and places of gathering. Fear of your child not succeeding and ending up in poverty leads to monitoring and managing your child's school performance. And of course, at the opposite end of over-managing your child's life is the age-old parental opiate – *denial*. Simply deny that anything is happening or, better yet, that it is even possible for any of these "bad" things to happen in my house, in this neighborhood, or to my children, and you have basically just renounced your connection to your child.

Now, what is the root cause of this worry? Why, in fact, do children take these paths, perceived by many of us to be negative, such as drug use and sexual experimentation at a young age? Many times the root cause, and the reason for the child's involvement in these activities, is the parent's fear itself. By having *fear* of your child doing something, you focus your energy on that thing. The child senses this fear. Perhaps it's a fear you've had for years. Consider this — if you have a fear of your child growing up to be a drug user, and if you've had this fear since your child was young, then how many times has the following thought passed through your mind: "I hope my child does not become a drug user." Thinking this thought *only once per day for 10 years means you have had this thought 3,650 times!*

What's the problem here? It's that the Universe does not understand the concept "not", because there is no negative at the highest source. The Higher Power only deals in positives and in reality; it simply "omits" that which it cannot understand, for polarity is like a foreign language at that level. Therefore, all the Universe hears from you, the parent, is "my child drug user". That's it. So thinking "I hope my child does not become a drug user" is *actually* like saying "my child drug user" 3,650 times to the Universe, and to the child through the mental telepathy of your child-parent bond. Understood this way, when the reality of the thoughts manifest, and your child becomes a drug user, you must then understand that *you had a part in actually creating this reality.*

Imagine, instead, if you said every day, "I hope my child becomes an enlightened person with an evolved spiritual perspective." In this case, the Universe hears "child enlightened spiritual perspective". Now, not only are you sending this intention to the Universe and your child, you will *unconsciously begin acting as if your child is that thing already*! In this way, you are aligning every fiber of your being to help your child manifest whatever they desire. Think about it – do people experiencing a state of spiritual evolution and enlightenment become drug addicts? This is impossible for their energy vibration is too high to let something like that into their lives. It will simply never come up for them. Focusing on the positive, instead of the fear and worry of the negative, is the *only way* to assist your child. By focusing on the fear and worry, you may actually move your child in the direction of experiencing that perceived "negative" reality.

Second, and equally important to understand, is that hiding your children from whatever you perceive as negative is not only ineffective in keeping your children from experiencing that thing, it may actually drive your child towards that reality. Why? Because, as much as we like to think it, parents are *not* perceived by the child as their primary life reflection tool after the pre-teen years. Typically it's the child's friends, or perhaps a hero of some sort, who take on that role. In addition, your child's soul is like a magnet, drawing everything they want and need to them, outside of your control. With the modern age of mass media and Internet, your child will get exposed to whatever it is you are trying to keep from them in due time any-

anyway. You simply cannot stop this, neither physically nor metaphysically.

The only thing you are doing by keeping that information from your child is making it more likely that they will make their decisions out of fear rather than knowledge. Either way, it is not as good a situation as if you, the parent, had allowed your child access to the information and sent an energy of acceptance toward the "taboo" subject.

Does this mean you should bring up every reality you perceive as negative with your child "just in case"? Not at all. What it does mean is this: if your child, either directly or indirectly, hints at a curiosity in any subject, you should nourish that curiosity, and encourage the child to learn more about it, and then give your own perspective. Sex, drugs, rock n' roll – no subject should be taboo because if your child brought it up to you, there is a *karmic reason* they need to deal with this subject. You see, our souls don't do anything randomly – does God do anything randomly? Therefore, your child has a good reason for bringing to you any taboo subject, even though it may not be apparent to you, or even your child, at the time.

Sound odd? It is a bit non-traditional. Let's say your child asks you about drugs because he heard something about it, and you encourage your child to research the subject. The child senses no fear from you on this subject, therefore it is not a "scary" subject. There is no doubt in your heart so the child is not intrigued by the mystery of doing something "behind closed doors" with regard to this subject.

Rather than fear, doubt and discipline, should your child make the inevitable decision to move towards that subject, you *accept* that your child wishes to learn more about this subject. You provide information for your child, all that you have at least, and you encourage him to seek out information from other sources, all that he will need to make his own decision. Yes, his own decision. Why do you fear this as a parent? In a few years, if your child is a teenager, she will have the ability to make this choice anyway, behind your back. What choice do you think your child will make in any case? Is she that vulnerable and irrational, that when provided with a coherent, deep understanding of the situation, and with no fear expressed by you, she will not make a decision that is in her best interest? Trust your child more.

You will soon not be there to guide them anyway. They are soon to be adults and they must make their own decisions in a few years, whether you like it or not. All you can do is assist them to connect with their higher selves when making important decisions. You simply won't be there to make the decisions for them very much longer anyway. The younger your children start learning to make intelligent, coherent decisions, *aligned with their higher selves*, the better off they will be in their later years.

And, even if they do need to experience something that you perceive as negative, because that experience is what their soul needs to grow and evolve, at least they are doing so without fear and have a total, complete understanding to their maximum level at that time. Indeed, by accepting your children's wisdom and instilling in your children the idea that they are individually 100% responsible for their own lives, rest assured that they will fulfill their higher purpose, whatever road that may take.

3 STEPS TO ACCEPTING MY CHILD

These affirmations may help during more trying times in learning to accept your child's life.

1 – "My child is being guided by his/her inner wisdom, and so s/he cannot make a wrong decision. My job is to accept my child's decisions. If I wish to help, I can start by connecting with my own inner wisdom, and thus providing my child a reflective tool to aid them in connecting with their higher self."

2 – "My child and I are co-teachers to each other in this lifetime. I will first respect my child's words and actions of wisdom as a way of reflecting onto him/her, so that they may later see the wisdom in my words."

3 – "I have gratitude towards my child for helping me to truly learn and understand of the energy of acceptance, even if it feels uncomfortable at first."

PART II
Parents as Guides

Chapter 6

A New Affirmation

In the previous section, we discussed that the power behind parenting is not discipline, it is guidance. The more enlightened perspective is to see yourself as a guide for your child, not a disciplinarian. So then, how can this be done? The truth is, as parents we intuitively know how to guide our children. We just need to remove the veil of confusion that has pervaded conventional parenting techniques and, at the same time, learn to trust the parental intuition we were all given when we incarnated on the earth plane. For remember, it was your soul's conscious choice to become a parent, and your soul is created from infinite universal intelligence. In this perspective, the intuitive understanding of raising a child is intrinsic in us and easily accessible, if we only knew where to look.

To make the transition from a parenting format based on discipline to one based on guidance, there are three key steps. The first and most important is for you, as the parent, to *acknowledge your child's divine right to self-rule.* Let's break this affirmation down piece-by-piece.

By "acknowledge" we mean to truly and fundamentally accept, but not acceptance in the way the word is usually used, which tends to leave out intention. By acceptance here we *do not* mean bowing to something's will that is outside of your control, because "that's just the way it is". Rather, we mean *conscious acceptance,* and this means coming to the understanding that what you are accepting was indeed created by you. The process of acknowledgement is bringing conscious acceptance into the forefront of your reality and then verbally honoring that conscious acceptance.

By "your child's divine right", we mean first acknowledging that your child is divine by his *very nature,* and not only when he acts in certain ways or accomplishes certain things. Indeed, your child's divinity is inherent in her very creation. Your child was created from the Higher Source and is still a part of that Higher Source, like all else in the universe, and so she is by nature a divine entity. Typically, in order to consciously and completely be able to acknowledge this, parents must first acknowledge their own divinity.

By saying your child's divine "right", we mean accepting the 100% complete control that your child's soul has, by universal right, over his current lifetime as your child on this Earth plane. Thus, we say it has been decreed by universal divinity that your child is a part of that which is divine, is hence divine herself, and has right of free will and conscious choice by virtue of that divinity.

The last portion, "to self-rule", is an acknowledgement that, because children by nature of their divinity have 100% control of their lives, this also means they must have 100% responsibility for their lives. For in the divine sense, power and responsibility are one. All actions in this Universe have an equal and opposite reaction – this is the most fundamental Natural Law in our dimension of reality. Therefore, there is no case when Power is given without its twin, Responsibility. So, if children have a divine right to self-rule, they also have the divine mandate of 100% responsibility for their own life situations.

This discussion leads us very naturally to the second step in the process, which is instilling true responsibility in your child. This step, indeed, is what discipline in the old paradigm was trying to accomplish. Where it came short was in not acknowledging, very simply, your child's divine right to self-rule.

For indeed if your child is 100% in control and 100% responsible for her own life, why does your child have parents? The people that, by virtue of one of the most fundamental actions in this dimension of our Earth plane (procreation), are tied to the child forever. If your child is connected to infinite universal intelligence, what role could the parents possibly have in helping the child grow and learn?

The answer is that, even though your child intuitively understands all this at the subconscious level, at the conscious level, he needs guidance in bringing this power and understanding into everyday reality.

Indeed, our modern society is, every day, teaching our children the exact opposite. Major societal institutions (school, church) are set up with an *external* punishment-and-reward system that belittles children's self-responsibility and disconnects our children from their intuitive and innate sense of self-responsibility. The biggest fallacy is that this is done under the guise of "teaching the child responsibility". As an example, let's take the school system's punishment and reward system. This system, based on an administrator's evaluation of our children's behavior, is supposed to instill responsibility in the child? Responsibility for what? For how the principal or authority figures, with their limited understanding of your child, feels about the child? This is idiotic — and dangerous. The entire school system, where children spend the majority of their time, is constantly reinforcing an external punishment-and-reward system based on right and wrong, disconnecting our children from their higher selves in the process. If you talk out of turn, the school takes away your recess time; if you behave, they give you an ice cream party. This continues on through college and even into the workplace. Good behavior is rewarded by the company, bad behavior is punished. And the cycle of control residing outside one's self perpetuates, allowing the masses to be controlled easily by manipulative authority figures.

Fortunately, the bond that emotional and physical energies create between child and parent necessarily means that your influence will be greater. So it doesn't matter if the schools, government, the TV and mass media, and even your Uncle Bob don't teach your children how to awaken self-responsibility within themselves. As long as you do, your child will learn it and become a more enlightened entity.

How can you teach this to your child? The first step is removing those mechanisms that create the veil of outside responsibility in your child. In other words, by choosing not to govern your relationship with your child based on systems and processes that reinforce a false sense of outside responsibility in your child, and instead choose to govern that relationship with processes that instill a sense of the true nature of your child's 100% self-responsibility.

One such system, talked about in the previous section, is traditional discipline. Just by removing discipline as the defining feature in the parent-child relationship will help immensely. It will be an enormous challenge, especially at first; but, isn't governing your relationship with your child using discipline already a huge challenge?

To help our children more, we as parents must learn to develop interactive tools with our children that instill and help awaken their natural sense of self-responsibility. One method to achieve this is directly stating it to your child – we give our children so little credit for understanding the deeper functioning of the universe. Recall that your child, by virtue of his age, is very likely closer to universal consciousness than you. They have spent less time separated from that consciousness in this lifetime than you (in mundane terms, they are "younger".) Therefore, simply explaining to your children that they are 100% responsible for everything they do by virtue of Natural Law in the Universe will work wonders.

You can also point this out to your child when she experiences it. Experience is truly the best teacher, and so, once your child sees this natural law inherently affecting her reality, her perspective will change and evolve quickly. So let's say your child falls and hurts his knee. Instead of "blaming" the fall on the ground or the stone your child tripped over, or stepping in immediately to kiss the bruise and "make it better", try another route. After comforting your child, ask your child why he chose to fall and hurt his knee, and experience this physical pain at this time? What is his soul trying to learn from this? Remind them they are 100% responsible for their actions. The stone did not "cause" them to trip any more than air "causes" them to breathe – it is their lungs in the latter case, their soul in the former case.

Indeed, the biggest challenge to instituting this system is letting go of fear and doubt as a parent, and allowing your child to make "mistakes". Let's look at an example. After reading this book, you are fascinated by the concepts and want to begin implementing these techniques and understandings into your everyday parenting routine. All goes well until you run into a situation where you previously had used discipline. Say your child was supposed to clean her room, but failed to do so in the time period set aside. What to do? The old way was to discipline the child, take something away or dole out punishment. But again, this takes the true responsibility for that action out of your child's hands.

Best thing to do – let your child experience what it is like to live in a dirty room! You can also explain to your child the concepts of 100% responsibility, her own divinity, and karmic consequence, but above all else, just let your child experience it. Something will happen, eventually. Perhaps they will lose an item that is of value to them due to the room being unorganized and messy, or they may take ill because their room's hygiene is poor and then miss a key social event or fun activity because of this, or hundreds more potential karmic reactions will occur. This reaction *must happen* because, again, for every action in this universe, there is an equal and opposite reaction.

When that reaction happens, your child is likely to be emotionally upset. Simply let your child experience those emotions, for that is his method of learning! Comfort him, but do not try to take away the pain or make up for the situation in any way. That is, after all, a situation he created through free will of choice, and without these "mistakes" or opportunities of inner learning, there is no way your child will be able to understand these concepts. In fact, it is better that they have small pains now rather than much larger pains by learning these lessons in adulthood where "mistakes" have a much bigger impact on life.

When your child is calmer, after going through this karmic experience, and without saying, "I told you so", you can again gently confirm the natural laws. Perhaps explain your understanding of why things occurred as they did but, even this, your child must eventually grasp intuitively.

Thus for parents to conceptualize themselves as their children's guides is really to say that we are, by nature, spiritual guides. For if your children could only connect to their higher selves, they can access all that knowledge and power that the high-

higher self has in order to complete their journey in this lifetime. There is no practical knowledge, as such, that the parent is obligated to teach. It may be that during the course of an emphasis on growing your child's self-consciousness, practical lessons are necessary. But try not to focus on any one piece of knowledge or information that you may feel inclined to impart as the parent. For, in the end, this is simply not your role. The focus is less on what you must "do" as a parent, and more on simply "being" a parent. This is the true way of enlightened parenting.

Chapter 7

The Parent-Child Soul Contract

Have you ever reflected upon the nature of your relationship with your child from a spiritual perspective? Your connection with your child takes the form of what is known as a soul contract. Soul contracts are agreements, much like contracts in business, made between two (or more) individuals that define the terms of a venture, relationship, or expedition.

A soul contract is made by and between 2 (or more) souls before incarnating onto the Earth plane to experience a physical lifetime. So, at the point in which our souls are in the Light plane, we choose to come to the Earth plane and experience a lifetime with a specific set of challenges, opportunities, and people in order to learn certain lessons and evolve spiritually. At the time of this choice, we also choose to make soul contracts with other souls who will, in tandem with us, experience a physical lifetime and grow and evolve together.

These soul contracts lay out the terms of the agreement – how we will be related to each other, what role we will play, how we will show up in each other's lives, etc. Sometimes, in order to learn a specific lesson and evolve, we will choose a soul contract with someone that, while on the Earth plane, will involve quite a painful relationship. For example, you may choose a soul contract with someone where they murder you in this lifetime in order that you learn not to fear death. Perhaps, through this experience, the other party learns the value of human life. It may sound harsh, but it happens all the time. Sometimes, this is the only way a particular soul can learn a particular lesson.

Indeed, think of your physical lifetime on this Earth as a play, and the important people in your life as your co-stars, and your higher selves as the writers, producers, and directors of the play. The only difference is that your lower selves as the actors don't know the lines in the play or what scene will come next. Only the directors know this. So the higher selves leave clues that the actors must pick up on in order to guide the play successfully into the next scene.

Armed with this understanding, we are ready to examine the child-parent soul contract.

We begin with the statement: *Every child chooses his/her parent, and every parent chooses his/her child.*

This is one of the most fundamental truths in parenting, and yet one of the hardest to grasp. How often have you said to yourself, perhaps in moments of utter frustration, "I wish my child were more/less_____." Reflecting back on your experiences growing up, how often have you said, "I wish my parents were more/less_____."

What is important to realize, as hard as it is for the conscious mind to accept, is that you chose your parents and they chose you – and that you chose to have parents with the specific traits, personalities, and views as your birth parents in this lifetime. This was, after all, your soul contract with them. Things were designed *by you* the way they are in order for you to evolve as a spiritual entity. Now, turn the tables and consider the same soul contract you had as a child with your parents; you are now standing on the other side of that bridge with your own child. And again, both of you have chosen this relationship in order to evolve as spiritual beings.

For example, is it possible that your child, perhaps as an infant, was overly fussy and didn't allow you to sleep at night for over a year? Is it possible that you chose this circumstance? Why would I, you ask? Although it is not obvious to the conscious mind, there is value in all of your child's actions and how they affect you, even if you perceive some as "negative." For example, perhaps your higher self wanted you to learn patience and, in past lives and other situations, which were easier mediums through which to learn this art, you were not able to do so. Knowing that you must learn patience in order to evolve spiritually, your higher self set up a situation with you as a parent of a fussy child so that you were almost *forced* into learning patience, albeit with a little bit of discomfort.

Magnify this example to every single interaction between yourself and your child, and you quickly see that the child-parent contract is one of the most involved and deepest soul contracts, because of the proximity the two souls typically share with each other over the course of a lifetime. This understanding should allow you, as the parent, to be less stressed. For, if all your child's actions are to help you learn, and indeed you chose a child with exactly the characteristics and personality of this particular child, even those points that your lower self perceives as negative, this naturally leads you to the following conclusions (and affirmations):

1.   I should accept my child's behavior because this is the exact behavior I need right now in order to learn a lesson that I have chosen to learn. I don't need to express excess anger or frustration, or blame my child in any way for his/her behavior.

2.   I will remind my child, and myself, that we are 100% responsible for our actions, and as such, we should strive for highest purpose to avoid paying karmic debts in the future.

3.   Indeed, perhaps if I pay attention and learn the lessons being presented to me, the behavior I regard as "undesirable" may naturally fall away, as the purpose of my child's behavior is likely for me to learn this lesson. As nothing in this universe exists without purpose, therefore if something loses its purpose, it will naturally lose its existence.

So having understood the inner workings of the child-parent soul contract, what is its purpose? Interestingly enough, this depends on both the child's and the parent's state of individual spiritual progress. For there are only two reasons that souls would choose to enter into a soul contract of any kind, especially a child-parent partnership soul contract. One is to cleanse built-up karma, and the other is to form a co-evolution unit. In almost all cases, there is a mixture of both in every parent-child relationship; the amount and emphasis is the cause for the majority of variation. Let's take each point individually.

- Cleansing past karma

Very simply, you have accumulated past karma with your child and, in the overwhelming majority of cases, there is some negative karma that needs cleansing between the two of you. And yes, this means that in past lives, at least at some point, you and your child have likely hurt each other very deeply. This is counterintuitive at first – how could I have hurt my child, if I love her so much, most parents would ask? However, it is just that feeling of love towards your child that your higher self wanted you to feel, for it will cleanse whatever hurt you have caused your child in past lives.

Think about it – what better way to teach a soul to love another soul than to make that soul the parent of the other soul? And this is exactly the case – the human emotion of parenthood is very close to unconditional love. So then, giving this feeling of unconditional love towards your child will naturally cleanse any past karma that you may have, and indeed, it may be a large part of the reason that you and your child chose this parent-child relationship. Your child's soul will now get to feel love from you, which may, unconsciously, cause her to forgive you for past life damages. You, on the other hand, will learn what it feels like to give love and cleanse your own soul of its scars. And, the opposite is almost always true as well – most children have a great amount of natural, unconditional love for their parents. And so, the karmic cleansing also works in reverse.

Indeed, to enter into a parent-child soul contract with another individual is, when implemented properly, one of the greatest healing paths that you could have chosen for yourself and your child. Honor this, cherish it, and show gratitude for it.

- Co-evolution

Moving past cleansing karma, one arrives at the second reason for the parent-child contract – evolving one's self spiritually. Here again, the parent-child relationship becomes paramount. For the parent-child relationship is the only close relationship that you choose at birth and *without conscious knowledge*. Your spouse you chose with conscious knowledge while on the Earth plane. Your friends, your teachers, employers, co-workers, were all chosen while you were a conscious entity on the Earth plane. But the relationship between parent and child is chosen at birth; upon your conception, your mother and father become your parents, and you, their child. Therefore, this decision was made prior to entering the Earth plane as a conscious entity.

Why is this relevant? Well, think of how important your relationship with your child must be for this lifetime, that both your souls took no risks, so to speak. As soon as your child incarnated as a living entity, he was immediately in close contact with you. This was not a chance meeting to fall in love as with a spouse, no serendipitous circumstances as with a friend or other relationship. This relationship was birth-given, and thus, your soul wanted to take no chances as to whether the conscious mind could navigate its way through the Earth plane to find your child. Rather, they were "dropped in your lap", spiritually speaking.

So, given this importance, great care must be taken to understand how you and your child can co-evolve. Co-evolution simply means the joint spiritual development of two or more entities as a result of their continued interaction with each other. Very likely, you and your child were meant to learn lessons together, and discover new things together – or said another way, to evolve spiritually due to the interaction of your energies on this Earth plane in this lifetime. While it is possible that this evolution may take drastic and sometimes uncomfortable paths, such as separation from your child for an extended period of time through a divorce or other situation, in most cases the co-evolution process is joyous.

The problem is that, if neither parent nor child is looking at the relationship with the intent to find co-evolution synergy, they instead tend to focus on more mundane matters and miss out on both the evolution and the natural joy that the relationship holds. Be wise – look for your co-evolution purpose with your child. After all, you both chose each other in this exact situation with a true purpose in this lifetime.

Chapter 8

Parental Obligations Redefined

So, your soul signed a contract with your child's soul; well then, if this is truly the case, you are likely asking yourself, "What terms and conditions did I agree to?" Or put more simply, "What the heck did I sign up for?!" Fortunately, you did not obligate yourself to impossible demands when you inked the spiritual papers, although your child may espouse this viewpoint with you at times!

While each soul contract is unique, the generalities of a child-parent soul contract are actually quite universal. They are, from the parent's perspective:

- Learn to love unconditionally
- Learn to give without expectation of return
- Learn to accept who your children are

Let's take each of these separately.

Learning to love unconditionally is perhaps the most difficult task. The reason for this is that our views on love are likely to be mired by years of relationship turmoil and the general effects of living in a modern society. Therefore, our adult perceptions of unconditional love may be lacking.

To truly love another unconditionally, we must first love ourselves unconditionally. How many of us can truly say that we do? Everything from that extra layer of fat we wish we didn't have, to the regret that we may not have been there enough for Uncle Charlie before his death, or feelings of guilt when we drive by a homeless person knowing our car is worth enough money to feed him and thousands of others for a year – all these remind us of our lack of love for ourselves.

But, again, the attempt is what's important, especially in relation to your child. So then, put simply, how can one attempt or strive towards unconditionally loving one's child? The easiest gauge of this complex affair is to always put love into the intention of every action and word you take with your child. What this means is, no matter what you are doing, how you are expressing yourself, whether you're making the "right" or "wrong" decision, etc., etc., do you truly have love in your heart as the intention behind that thought/verbal expression/action? Ask yourself this; catch yourself in the most trying moments of struggle with your children. "Is my intent to express love for this wonderful being I call my child?" Perhaps even keep a log or a diary of events, noting which ones you felt were love-intended and which weren't. Over time, try to improve upon the love-based intentions.

Indeed, it will take time – and, depending on the level of love energy you as the parent have been able to accumulate during your adult lifetime, the levels of love expression you can provide your child will vary. But if the root intention is present, your child's soul will know. And really, children are not that demanding after all. In those soft moments of parenting intimacy when your children look up at you and say "Mommy / Daddy I love you" or some other sweet sentence, you realize intuitively that simply intending unconditional love towards your child is really and truly the only obligation you have as a parent.

The second point, **learning to give without the expectation of return,** is less touchy-feely, involving less heart energy, but rather much more pragmatic, involving mental or brain energy. However, this doesn't mean the smarter you are, the easier it will be to manifest this! It means you must focus and, at times, struggle with your thoughts as opposed to your feelings. Typically, each of us is usually better at one or the other. So if the unconditional love part sounded easy, this will likely be harder, and vice versa.

We say "learning to give" because indeed the emphasis is not lost on the word *learning*, for giving is a *learned behavior*. This may seem counter-intuitive at first. You might think it's easy to give something — you just hand over that object to another person. But, in deeper reality, the above reference is not giving at all. It is simply an exchange.

An *exchange* becomes *giving* only when the giver *loses all expectation of any return* on the exchange. Does this mean the giver is never compensated for the gift? Quite the opposite – by giving without the expectation of return, you actually draw higher and greater levels of compensation to you through the coalescence of your giving energy patterns in the universe. But then, the key word here is expectation. It is the *expectation of receiving a return* that muddies the exchange and moves it away from giving, not the reality of whether or not you actually receive a return.

But how is this so? It lies in the feeling of intention that you provide the receiver when you give or exchange something. When you truly *give* something to someone, they are charged, they are energized, and they feel great. Why? Because something has been provided to them without any expectation, "no strings attached." Furthermore, the intense love-wave generated by an act of giving is so powerful that it literally brightens up the room and that person's day.

We have all felt this in our adult lives in those sometimes elusive, genuine acts of kindness that another human being has bestowed upon us, when it just really "made our day". Perhaps a co-worker you never considered a close friend sent you flowers when you were ill, without any intention of political maneuvering other than genuine concern for your physical health. Or, maybe it was as simple as an impromptu neck massage by your spouse, just when you really needed it and direct from his/her heart.

This is true giving and, once you experience it, you can just "feel it" when it happens, and when you are engaged in true giving. So, how does this apply to our children? In the most basic way.

The general, overall, and all-encompassing feeling you provide to your child as *the basis of your entire relationship must be true giving*. Put simply, you cannot have any expectations of return from your child. Expect nothing now or in the future when you are older, not for them to accomplish things you missed out on in your life, not to brag about your child's Harvard education or piano virtuosity to your friends, and so on. Think about this deeply, for it is a thinking activity. When have you had thoughts, which perhaps led to actions that were not rooted in true giving towards your child? When have you expected something, anything, no matter how small, from them in return for all that you give them as parents?

Identify those times, and shift your mental effort into true giving. For one of the greatest damages you can do to your child is to violate this most fundamental substance of the parent-child contract. Why? Because, by not giving unconditionally, you must be doing the opposite (in our dualistic world); so you are, in fact, burdening your child with expectation. And this, of course, leads to enormous mental and emotional trauma for your child, for your child loves you unconditionally. So instead of focusing on their own lives, they begin to think, "mommy or daddy needs me." Being children, they do not know the boundaries of love, so they will sacrifice themselves and their lives, sometimes even literally, in order to pay back this expectation of return they feel from you.

Liberate your child instead by allowing them to feel your unconditional giving, and yet have no expectation of return. How will this make your child feel? Exactly – they will want and desire, not out of obligation, but out of their heart-felt love, to reciprocate to you, perhaps by striving to hold up their end of the child-parent contract to the utmost possible. This motivates you to give further, which further motivates your child, etc., etc.

And now, instead of the crushing cycle of debt, payback and expectation, you have created the up-lifting cycle of love, inspiration, and joy with our child. And you create a miracle in the process.

The final point, **learning to accept who your children are,** is a subject broached by many conventional parenting guides.

Typically, the issue is brought up in the context of the teenage rebellion stage of a child's growth cycle. While helpful to some degree, these guides typically do not come from a base understanding of what acceptance is. Because, before you can learn to accept who your children are, do you not first need to learn what true acceptance is?

True acceptance is not simply tolerance of an unwanted event, as is commonly thought, nor is it a resignation to "that's just the way it is." Rather, true acceptance is reaching the understanding that whatever circumstance exists, *it is in your best interest, aligned with your destiny, and helping you to achieve your higher purpose* on this earth. Or in simple terms, "it's all good."

Now, this commonly used phrase is actually a reminder in our most desperate hours that whatever is happening must be in our own best interest. But let's get a little more scientific. How exactly is everything in our best interest? It certainly doesn't feel that way during big things like the loss of a job or loved one, to little things like stubbing our toe in the morning in just that exact way to get on our nerves.

Well, getting back to a theme touched on earlier in the text, everything that happens is in our best interest because *we make everything happen* in our own lives. Whether directly by action/reaction, or indirectly via our thoughts and soul processes, our lives are one big play and we are the director, producer, and theatre owner all in one. We may not consciously be aware of this fact but, nonetheless, it is the truth at the most basic levels of life, from which all life springs.

So, if our higher selves, souls, or unconscious minds are creating all of our life's circumstances, why do "bad" things happen? Or should we say, why do we make "bad" things happen to us? The fundamental issue here is that it is our lower or Earth-bound selves that give the events their coloration into "bad" and "good", "positive" and "negative." It is our lower or Earth-bound selves that live in this world of duality. In the higher dimensions of existence, where your child just spent time prior to incarnating on this Earth (that's why newborns have that special "glow"), there is no duality. "Right" and "wrong", "bad" and "good", "positive" and "negative" simply don't exist. What does exist there? Reality or energy exists, pure and simple, untainted and un-judged by any coloration of duality.

So, it is the lower self that interprets these pure events and gives them coloration into dualistic components such as good and bad. It is sort of like the white light reflected through a prism; the prism provides the coloration. The reality is not those colors. Therefore, reality is pure, the sum of all dualities existing simultaneously and in harmony. However, our selective interpretation of certain events, much like a prism's selective interpretation of strands of color contained in white light, gives an incomplete understanding of that reality, and causes us to divide things into right and wrong, much like the prism divides light into red, blue, etc.

What's the next step? Well, by connecting with our higher selves, if even for an instant, we can begin to view our life's circumstances as pure light, and remove the colorations into dualistic concepts that tint our vision of deeper reality. We've all had these moments when a "flash" of light (quite literally, it seems) strikes us, some nugget of wisdom seemingly from the beyond provides instant insight or a path to greater serenity with whatever issue we are facing. Through varying types of meditative and intuitive practices, this ability can be refined — but that is a subject for another book.

Coming back from the esoteric, how does this all apply to parenting? Well, it comes back to the concept of acceptance. If we truly accept that we have created all our life's circumstances, and that we are very likely only seeing a partial picture, then we must accept that:

1 – We have ourselves created whatever issue we are currently having with our children.

2 – We are very likely only seeing a partial picture of our child's expression and what is truly happening in their lives.

Taking point 1 first, does it not then seem that, in any disagreement, argument or larger issue with our children, that we must first take responsibility for it, because indeed, have we not created this ourselves? A simple affirmation, "I accept that I have created this issue/situation/conflict with my son/daughter", would be a huge step. Read it again, say it, do it. It will make a huge difference. Uttering these words, out loud and repeatedly if possible (but at first, not necessarily in the presence of your child), is part of the process of connecting with your higher self and the higher dimensions of consciousness. This, in turn, will cause more "flashes of brilliance" to come your way regarding whatever issue spurred all this in the first place. Now, we are moving towards true *acceptance*.

At more advanced levels, uttering these words out loud to your child, even in mid-argument before they stomp out of the room and shut their door with the proverbial "I hate you!" teenage yell, will work wonders. Just look them in the eye and say, "I accept that I have created this issue/situation/conflict with you; this situation is my responsibility."

Now, some of you may be asking, "But what about my child's role in this?! Aren't they equally responsible?" The answer to this question is more complicated than it seems.

In short, no, they are not responsible, *if* the frame of reference is your reality. In the frame of reference of *their* reality and consciousness experience on this Earth plane, *they are 100% responsible.* How can this be, you may ask? You mean, both parties are 100% responsible, and yet neither is, at the same time? Sounds funny, and is very difficult for the dualistic mind to understand, but this is absolutely the truth. The reason? Each person's perceptive reality is, for intensive purposes, *the reality.* At least, this is how our lower selves work. At higher levels of consciousness, all these realities are seen as just reflective elements or "colors," if you will, of the unified One Reality, or white light.

But getting back to the parenting example – you may ask, if I take 100% responsibility for the situation with my child, won't that just encourage them to blame everything on me, and never take responsibility for themselves? While conventional wisdom may seem so, in fact this is the opposite from the truth.

Your child intuitively knows that they are 100% responsible in their higher levels and states of consciousness, but what has happened is that some

Earth plane event has caused him/her to get caught in a lower-self issue. This lower-self mind-set has then caused discomfort, leading to anger or sadness, and likely to the root cause of the internal issue that created the current external problem you are dealing with.

So, if you, as the parent, open yourself to your higher levels of consciousness, and declare to your child "I accept that I am 100% responsible for this situation, and that I have created this conflict with you," it accomplishes two things. First, it is leading by example – you are showing your child what it looks like to connect to higher levels of consciousness. Your naturally perceptive child will, at this point, be encouraged to do the same thing, if not consciously, then, subconsciously at least. Think about it – whenever you are in a room with a happy person, don't you find yourself feeling happier, or at least inclined to feel this way? Positive energy is contagious. In fact, scientific studies that measure brain wave activity have established that a positive thought actually carries 1,000 times the energy of a negative one. As you emanate the positive energy of connecting with your higher self, your child will naturally do the same, for you are both bound together in the eternal soul link as parent and child. Did you not, if you are a Mother, carry this being within your physical body for nine months? Did you not, if you are the Father, create this child from substance matter of your own physical body? Did this child not spring from the very DNA of your physical structure?

The second thing this type of statement does is completely defuse the situation, and completely confuse your child's over-emotional or over-active lower self. In that moment of confusion, when the lower self can't throw back the next insult, can't keep dwelling on hate and anger, the lower self will short-circuit. And, in that moment of short-circuit, your child's lower self cannot act, and therefore her higher self will come through, even if on the surface she just says "what-everrrrrrrrr" and storms off. Something has happened; there is a different stimulus in the environment, and your child will feel it. Perhaps they will talk to their friends, saying "My mom/dad did the weirdest thing today. We were arguing, and s/he stopped, and said that s/he was 100% responsible for the argument or some weird thing like that!" They may even mock you to their friends, but the important thing is they repeated it out loud! As many times as your child thinks about or repeats this, he is duplicating that flash of brilliance that he received the instant you started acting from higher levels of consciousness instead of your mundane lower-self.

Third, and most importantly, your affirmation as an enlightened parent will change your behavior towards your child. It will give you a liberating feeling, remind you that you are in control of your life and your situation. It will make you a calmer, happier parent, as well as have a wondrous effect on your children while assisting them with their internal conflicts and issues.

Now, what if the source of the issue is not a problem or conflict, but rather just a difference in who you are, how you think, and who your child is? In this case, instead of being angry and wondering why you and your child don't share more in common, you should be thanking your child for showing you a different perspective, for *trying to teach you acceptance*. Taking this perspective will cause your soul to grow.

You see, let's get back to a subject approached in the beginning of this section. Recall that you and your child, when residing in higher dimensions prior to materializing on this Earth, scripted this entire lifetime together and agreed on the "play". You are in a play, where you are co-directing and co-acting and co-producing with your child. You just don't realize it.

So let's say your child is a gothic punk-rocker, or hangs out with a "tough" crowd, or engages in drug use, or their sexual orientation is not to your liking, etc. And you love fine wine, Mozart concerts, and walks on the beach by moonlight (stereotypes, I know, but to make a point). An impossible match? Hardly. In fact, the most likely situation is that you and your child *chose* to incarnate on this Earth as opposite personalities, in order to teach each other acceptance. If this is the case, it is actually a *blessing* that you and your child are this different. Why? Because if your child wasn't your polar opposite, what would you need to accept? And therefore, how would you learn the concept of acceptance, so that your soul could grow?

Given this perspective, you should be *thanking* your child for being different from you, for it is in this very aspect that he/she is most valuable to you. Indeed, it is what you "signed up for" when you created your child–parent soul partnership contract. It is what you requested your child to do prior to incarnating together on this earth for this lifetime cycle. How then, can you get angry or upset at your child for doing what you asked them to do in the first place?

Thank your children, to yourself, and, when you are ready, even thank them directly, out loud, for being different and for all the things they are doing to teach you the wonderful and infinitely valuable concept of acceptance.

In the end, you're not going to change your children anyway. The more you try, the more you resist learning acceptance, then the more your children will go in a direction that's different from you. You signed up to learn this lesson, why make the lesson so much harder on yourself? Your children are being guided by their higher spiritual selves, by God, even if it doesn't seem like it at times. Who are you to judge their paths? How could you possibly know what events and experiences your child's unique and infinite soul needs to learn on this Earth in order to evolve? You can't, and it's not your job anyway. Your job is to accept, support, and love them, in whatever incarnate form they take, in *whatever* path they choose, no matter how "bad" or "negative" you think it is. If they come to you directly for advice, and if you feel obliged to give advice without coming from a place of low energy, then by all means give it. Otherwise, stick to your lessons, and let your child learn his or hers.

Another subject to approach in this section is projecting onto your child. Parental projection is one of the most difficult problems for many of us to overcome, and thus the subject warrants some discussion. Since this subject has been dealt with somewhat adequately by conventional parenting guides, it will only be touched upon here.

In short, projecting onto your child involves the act of expecting something from your child to make up for one of your personal needs, unfulfilled desires or goals. In essence, it is the externalization of your internal desires and qualities onto your child.

Given the close relationship between parent and child, projecting usually happens unconsciously, making it that much harder, of course, to notice and correct. In addition, it is very unlikely that your child will be able to notice your projections, except at an older age, when often the proverbial "damage" has been done. Thankfully, self-regulation of this behavior is quite easy, given some basic spiritual and meditative practices.

The first step, very simply, is to give without expectation, which was covered earlier in this text. If the parent stays firmly within this mindset, the possibility of projection becomes extremely low. However still, the key to identifying projection is to ask yourself as the parent, "Do I have any personal motivation or desire for my child to do/act/be this thing that I'm thinking about? Or is this truly a selfless issue, focused 100% on my child?"

And this, of course, is the key. Our children are *not* there to fulfill the desires we missed out on during our lifetime, nor are we meant to live our lives vicariously through our children. In addition, our children are completely unique entities, and their experiences will also be 100% unique. Therefore, there is no need to transfer our fears, doubts and worries to our children, even as a proverbial "heads up" to life, because their experiences as an incarnate being on this Earth plane will be 100% and completely unique and their own.

PART III

Your Child's Higher Self Intentions

Chapter 9

Meet Your Child's Higher Self

The final chapter of this journey will focus on, not coincidentally, the final step in spiritual parenting: assisting your child in connecting with his/her higher self. Indeed, if your entire parenting aura was focused on assisting your child in connecting with her higher self, you would be the perfect parent, for what you need to be. All the other stuff would just be preparation. This simple and, at the same time, not so simple orientation for your parenting will not only change your relationship with your child, it will change the world.

The most important thing to understand about assisting your child in connecting with his higher self is that your child already has the natural inclination to do so, as we all do. Therefore, your job, in some sense, is already halfway done! The key to spiritual parenting is identifying your child's higher-self intentions and then nurturing them, or said another way, assisting them or guiding them.

What is a higher-self intention? Very simply, it is the outward manifestation, through words, actions, feelings, etc. of your child's inner intention to connect with his higher self. The first step, therefore, in assisting your child is to be able to identify the higher-self intention behind the thought /action/feeling that your child is expressing.

How does one do this? Very simply, by evaluating and understanding, first, and foremost, what it feels like to have a higher-self intention yourself. Again, a subject for another book, but assuming you are there, you will be able to "feel" your child's higher-self intention behind their outward manifestation. In fact, even if you don't have such a grand frame of reference for your own life, simply by cleansing your parental aura, given the techniques discussed earlier in this text, your intuitive understanding will increase, and it will naturally become easier to sense your child's higher-self intentions.

Affirm to yourself that you already know all you need to know to be a great parent. Ask for guidance within yourself and look for the guidance to show up in your life. Believe that you are a perfect parent for what you need to be, and you will begin to see the guidance manifesting throughout your parenting life.

One practical way to identify a higher-self intention is to examine its polar opposite, the empty or lower-self intention. Typically, these are outward manifestations that come from a place of anger, sadness, depression, guilt, hopelessness, etc. In some way, whenever your child's manifestation *does not* involve any of these root intentions, it's probably a higher-self intention.

Another good gauge is that anything involving creativity is typically a higher-self intention. This is not limited to "artistic creativity", though it often takes that form. It could be creativity in different, more subtle ways. Let's say a child is extremely creative, even to the point of becoming irritating, in terms of how to perform a simple task such as a bedtime routine. The child plans and re-plans a complex routine for going to bed at night, always adding a new note of creativity. Instead of becoming upset that the child is "taking too long" and missing her bedtime, engage your child's imagination. Go into the world of the creative bedtime routine with them and find where the higher-self intention is. Remember, your child is created perfectly and all creation has purpose; without purpose, a thing would not exist. Therefore, there is purpose to your child's elaborate bedtime routine plans, so respect it and understand your child.

Further, any thought or action your child has towards self-improvement, new learning, new ways of thought, or self-development and evolution are coming from a higher purpose intention. It is less important to pinpoint what it is exactly that your child wants to learn or delve into; it is more important to respect and understand how and why your child chooses to enter into this path. This is where the parent's task is *non-judgment*. Many times, a child will come to a parent and ask to learn something, or show an interest in learning something that, on the surface, may seem at best useless or at least peculiar to the parent. The parent in this case may deny the child's interest, or at least not support it fully. What if your child came to you one day and said she wanted to learn alchemy, the study of how to turn ordinary metal into gold? How would you take to such a request? Would you think that your child's imagination is running wild with something they must have seen in a cartoon, or would you sit down with your child and Google the word "alchemy" and start on this spiritual journey with your child? Ask yourself this truly, for many other and different examples could be be used, examples as varied as the stars and planets in the universe itself.

Remember that any inkling or thought that your child has about a certain action as self-evolution is an alarm signal for a higher intention purpose behind that action, even if your child is merely teaching himself what a higher intention purpose is. Don't be so worried about results or outcomes; learn to enjoy the process instead. Clear your mind, your heart, and your parental aura of everything except unconditional love for your child, and you will be all your child needs.

The other general category of assistance you can provide your child is to guide her in clearing blockages that may hinder her connection with the higher self. And in truth, helping your child to actually identify the blockage may be the most valuable first step. From there, your child will usually find her own way.

What is a blockage to spiritual progress? Essentially it is a lower-self intention that is creating an emotion such as anger, depression, or anxiety that then "clogs" the connection of your child with his higher self. It is like a clogged artery (and, it can literally lead to one) keeping blood from pumping properly to and from the heart.

So powerful are these emotions, in fact, that they are the basis of so-called "black magic" and other dark occult occurrences. If form follows thought, then it would reason that negative forms would follow negative thoughts. Indeed, the sorcery of old can very simply be replicated in the modern era by focusing a strong intention through a relatively clear medium at a constant rate on a specific subject, be it positive or negative.

Therefore, your child's anger, sadness, anxiety or greed is a clear sign that the connection with the higher self has become corroded. Indeed, this is the root purpose of all these so-called "negative" emotions. The "negative" emotions are not simply there to make your child, or you, feel uncomfortable. They are, rather, more of a sign, a compass pointing in a direction that indicates that something is not aligned here. It is the manifestation of imbalance and, therefore, is intended to be a guide to let each of us know that perhaps we need to look at something more closely. Usually the thing in question is the very thing about which we are feeling this negative emotion. If we feel angry about something, there is a root cause to this anger – not something to "resolve", per se, but a metaphor. The situation that made us angry is often a metaphor for a larger blockage, and so the anger acts as a finger pointing us in the right direction. The same goes with your child.

For the connection of your child with his higher self is a two-way street. Information is sent to the higher self in the form of a request or affirmation, and wisdom and guidance are sent back down from the higher self for use in manifesting intentions within the material plane. So when this communication system gets corroded, your child will receive half-signals, mixed signals, or no signals at all. Imagine it is like a radio wave; as you get "out of range", there is static, and then the signal fades out. Without these signals from our higher selves, the lower selves begins to take over and guide us. In this situation, the guidance is prone to be of lower value.

For any individual aligned with his higher purpose and in touch with his higher self ceases to exhibit such emotions and negative thoughts naturally. This is not because of trying to "stamp out" these emotions, which will only make them stronger, but rather because the glass is full, so to speak, with something else – namely inspiration. There is no room for any other thought form to enter the full cup.

The single most important thing you can do to guide your child in this respect is to make yourself a mirror of higher-self reflection. Every time you succumb to "negative" emotions, you are showing your child what it looks like to have a lower-self intention. By contrast, every time you overcome your urge to display negative emotions and instead deal with a problem using a higher-self intention, you are reflecting to your child what it looks like to have a higher-self intention.

The ramifications of this, while simple, are extraordinary. In every situation that arises with your child, try to utilize a higher-self intention. Keep a diary of it, and see your improvements over time. It is the single greatest gift you can give to your child.

EPILOGUE

I find it more appropriate to use the term Epilogue at the end of this text than Conclusion, for there is truly no conclusion to the infinite journey of parenting, only steps in its continued evolution. Remember that, no matter what you do, whether you follow the guidance in this text or not, you are still contributing to that evolution in your own manner.

Therefore, as we said at the outset, all parents throughout the world are linked and bonded, simply by virtue of this wonderful experience that we have all chosen. Be blessed, go forth and enjoy this rich experience.

Peace and oneness.

LaVergne, TN USA
29 April 2010
181021LV00001B/24/P